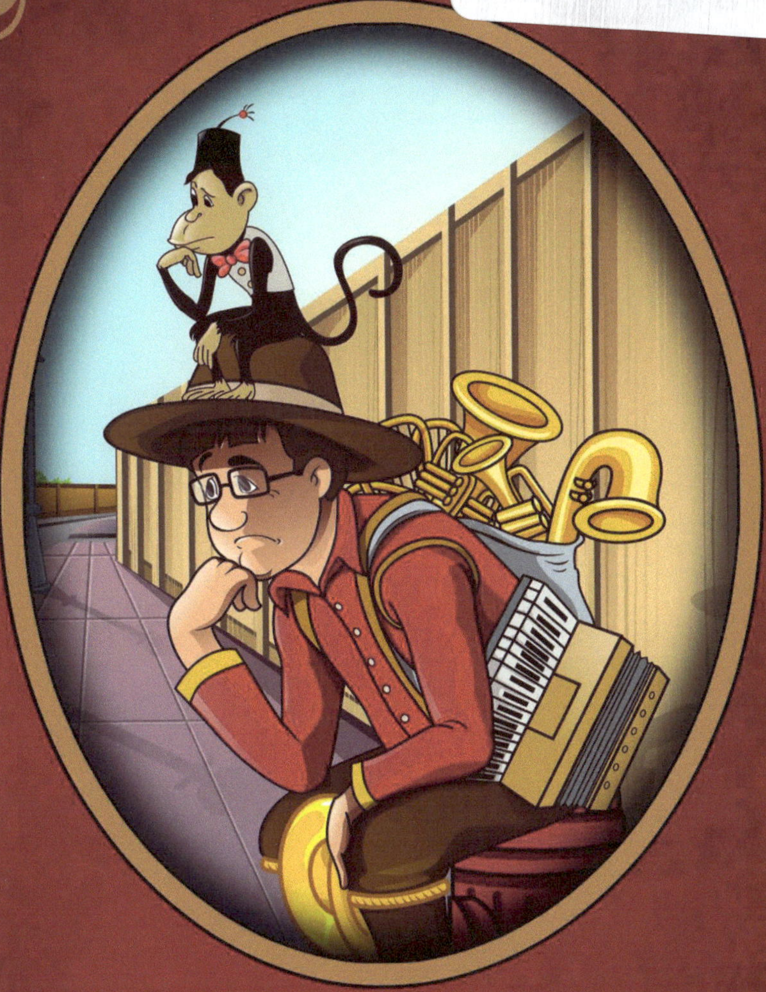

The Town That Didn't Speak

Written by ZaZa

Illustrated by Dream Computers
Produced by MRPwebmedia

The Town That Didn't Speak

There once was a town,
where nobody spoke,
not a sentence, a syllable,
not even a joke.

It created confusion,
but what could you do?
It's the way it was done.
It's all that they knew.

They'd go to the baker,
they'd point and they'd wave.
That's just how they it did it.
That's how they behave.

It wasn't efficient,
it wasn't so right.
But that's how they did it,
all day and all night.

Then came a fellow,
an ordinary bloke.

Who asked all the people,
he asked all the folk.

Does nobody talk?
Does nobody speak?
You just stand there and wave
to explain what you seek?

You go to the baker,
you point and you wave.

You don't get what you want,
that's not how to behave.

There once was a town,
where nobody spoke,
It wasn't so good;
it wasn't a joke.

Till a wise old stranger walked into town.

He noticed the people.
He noticed the frown.

"What's the problem?"
He said in his kind, gentle voice.
"Why don't you speak,
have you no choice?"

But the people all shrugged,
they had nothing to say.
It just wasn't them;
it wasn't their way.

There once was a town,
where nobody spoke,
Not a sentence, a syllable,
not even a croak.

Then a traveling musician arrived on the scene.

Wondering why everyone acted so mean.

So he thought and he thought about what could be done.

Perhaps they could sing, perhaps that'd be fun.

So he pointed and waved
at a bird in the sky.

And the people all nodded,
it was how they reply.

There once was a town,
where nobody spoke,
Not a sentence, a syllable,
not even a joke.

Then all of a sudden
a racket was heard.
They say it all started
with the sound of a bird.

The End

The Town That Didn't Speak

There once was a town, where nobody spoke,
Not a sentence, a syllable, not even a joke.

It created confusion, but what could you do,
It's the way it was done. It's all that they knew.

They'd go to the baker, they'd point and they'd wave,
That's just how they it did it. That's how they behave.

It wasn't efficient, it wasn't so right,
But that's how they did it, all day and all night.

Then came a fellow, an ordinary bloke,
Who asked all the people, he asked all the folk.

Does nobody talk? Does nobody speak?
You just stand there and wave to explain what you seek?

You go to the baker, you point and you wave.
You don't get what you want, that's not how to behave.

There once was a town, where nobody spoke,
It wasn't so good; it wasn't a joke.

Till a wise old stranger walked into town,
He noticed the people. He noticed the frown.

What's the problem? He said in his kind, gentle voice.
Why don't you speak, have you no choice?

But the people all shrugged, they had nothing to say.
It just wasn't them; it wasn't their way.

There once was a town, where nobody spoke,
Not a sentence, a syllable, not even a croak.

Then a traveling musician arrived on the scene,
Wondering why everyone acted so mean.

So he thought and he thought about what could be done,
Perhaps they could sing, perhaps that'd be fun.

So he pointed and waved at a bird in the sky.
And the people all nodded it was how they reply.

There once was a town, where nobody spoke,
Not a sentence, a syllable, not even a joke.

Then all of a sudden a racket was heard,
They say it all started with the sound of a bird.

The End!

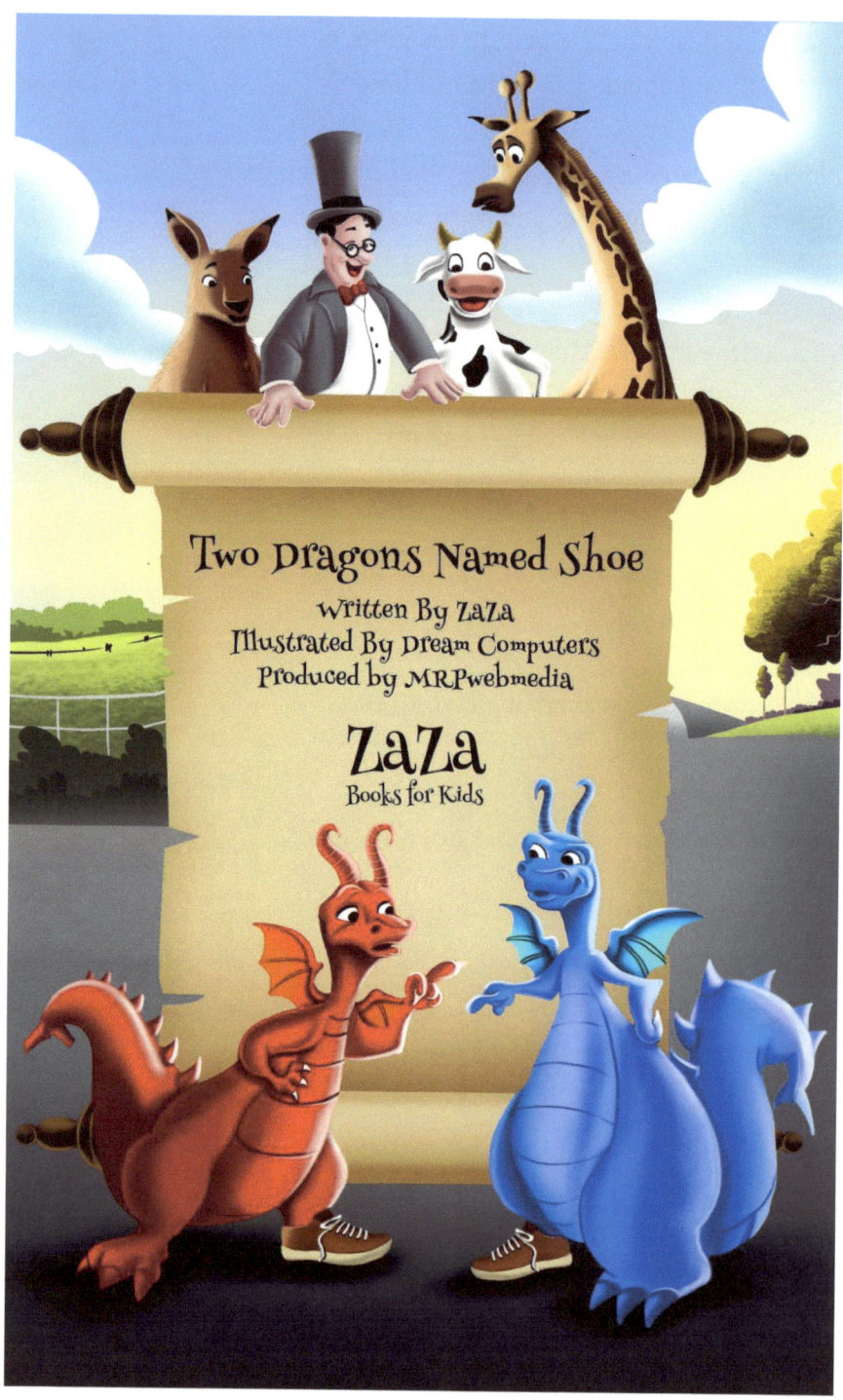

Two Dragons Named Shoe
eBook Version: http://bit.ly/1T7NM0e
Soft Cover: amzn.to/1XD80p7

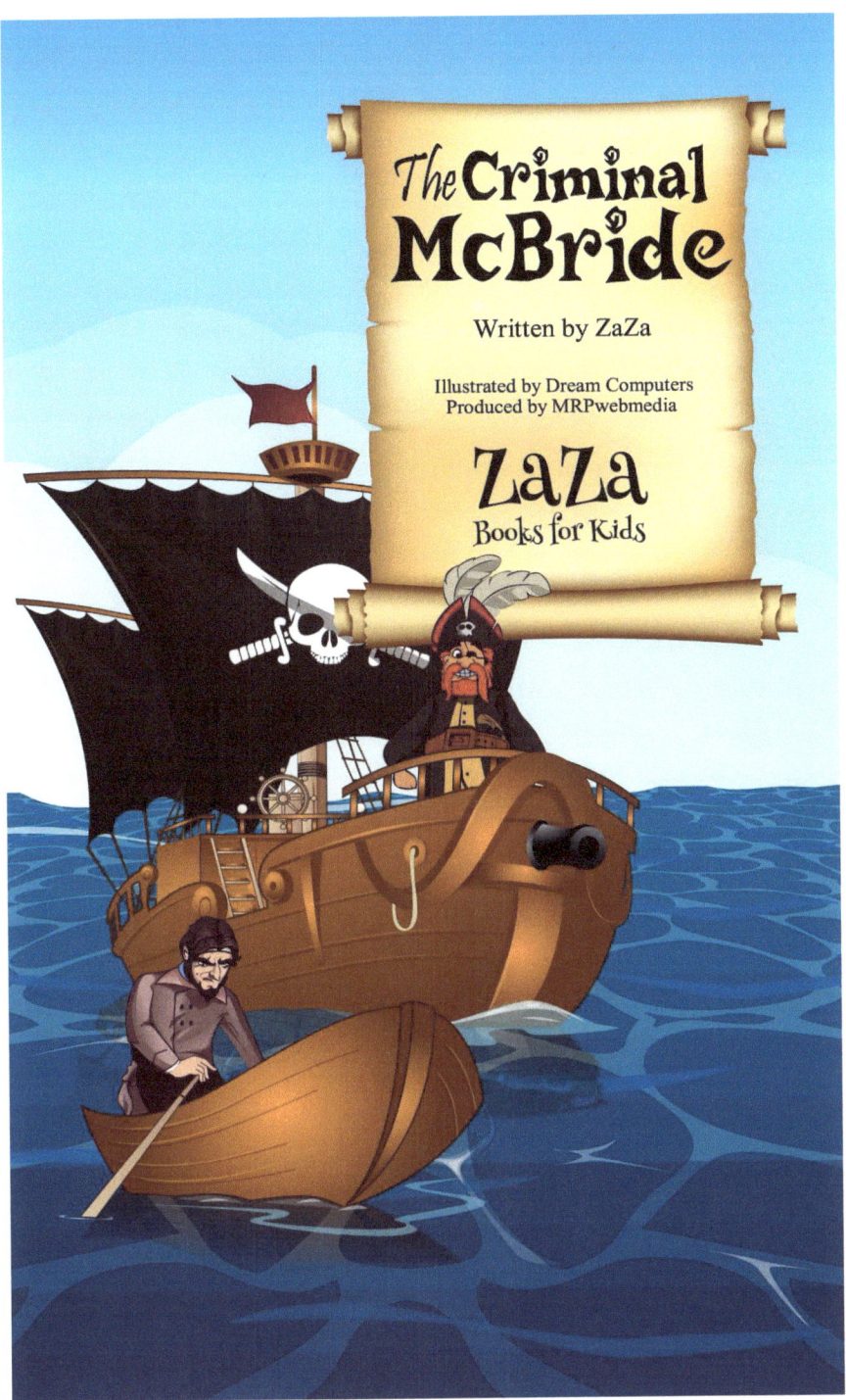

The Criminal McBride
eBook Version: http://bit.ly/29ZhSGw
Soft Cover: amzn.to/2ay3kgP

www.ingramcontent.com/pod-product-compliance
Lightning Source LLC
Chambersburg PA
CBHW042059290426
44113CB00001B/21